Faith Works

A Pocket Guide to Spiritual Growth

This book is the property of

_____

Address/phone

_____
_____
____   ____   _____

Dedication

This book is dedicated to the staff, volunteers and supporters of the
SOUTH COAST GOSPEL MISSION

notes

Table of Contents

Part One – The Things of God
- Chapter One — God — 9
- Chapter Two — The Word of God — 21
- Chapter Three — The Son of God — 27
- Chapter Four — The Spirit of God — 31
- Chapter Five — The Children of God — 35

Part Two – Growing in God
- Chapter Six — Add to Your Faith… — 47
- Chapter Seven — Goodness — 49
- Chapter Eight — Knowledge — 53
- Chapter Nine — Self-Control — 57
- Chapter Ten — Perseverance — 61
- Chapter Eleven — Godliness — 65
- Chapter Twelve — Brotherly Kindness — 67
- Chapter Thirteen — Love — 71
- Chapter Fourteen — The Reason — 75

Part Three – Other Matters
- Chapter Fifteen — Prayer — 79
- Chapter Sixteen — Bible Reading — 83
- Chapter Seventeen — Bible Memorization — 87
- Chapter Eighteen — Church — 91
- Chapter Nineteen — Work — 95
- Chapter Twenty — Money Matters — 97
- Chapter Twenty-one — Cults — 99
- Chapter Twenty-two — Spiritual Breathing — 101
- Chapter Twenty-three — Baptism — 103
- Chapter Twenty-four — Backsliding — 105
- Chapter Twenty-five — Two-step Discipleship — 109
- Chapter Twenty-six — Future Things — 111

notes

Part One

The Things of God

Does God even exist? If He does exist, does He care about you? This section is designed to help you understand what you believe about God and what difference it makes or should make in your life.

Only fools say in their hearts, "There is no God."
Psalm 53:1

*Anyone who wants to come to Him
must believe that God exists and that
He rewards those who sincerely seek Him.*
Hebrews 11:6

Chapter One

GOD

We should not approach the subject of God lightly. If God exists then we should try and discover and understand as much about Him as possible. There are good reasons for contemplating God's existence. Christians have rational reasons for their faith and have a rational faith. All people should examine the basis of their belief or non-belief in God. There are consequences of both belief and unbelief. This chapter is an attempt to reveal some of those consequences. As we look at the alternative viewpoints of God in a reasonable and clear format, we will also look at the logical outcome of each position.

Does God Exist?

To begin our discussion at the most basic level then we must start by stating a crystal clear fact. *Either God exists or He does not exist.* There can

FAITH WORKS

be no middle ground. There is no other alternative. Of course there are conclusions that must be formed as a result of either stance, but one stance or the other must be correct. We can demonstrate it like this:

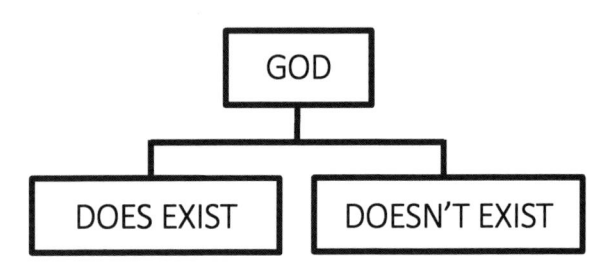

```
         ┌─────────┐
         │   GOD   │
         └────┬────┘
      ┌──────┴──────┐
┌───────────┐  ┌──────────────┐
│ DOES EXIST│  │ DOESN'T EXIST│
└───────────┘  └──────────────┘
```

Simple reason demands that one of these conclusions is the correct one. We will look at each side of the argument logically and see what we can discover. Let's begin by taking the shorter path. The path that says that God does not exist. I say shorter because there are not as many things to consider if there is no God.

┌─────────────────────┐
│   THERE IS NO GOD   │
└─────────────────────┘

CHAPTER ONE – GOD

If God does not exist then there can be no design or purpose for you as a person or mankind and creation as a whole. Life is simply what you make it. Right and wrong is not established or determined by God but by each individual or society. There is no God to help you while you live or to judge you after you die. The ultimate goal of life becomes self-satisfaction. An afterlife is conceivable but any knowledge of it would be a product of someone's supposed death experience. In short, if there is no God, you had better grab all the enjoyment you can get right here, right now because this moment is all you have.

If God Does Exist

Now let's look at the possible paths that people can travel if God does exist. Some of the paths will not be very different as far as the outcomes. But we need to travel down each path separately for the moment. First then is a glance at the possible alternatives when a person concedes that God exists:

FAITH WORKS

```
        ┌─────────────┐
        │  GOD EXIST  │
        └──────┬──────┘
       ┌───────┴───────┐
┌──────────────┐  ┌──────────────┐
│ HAS GIVEN US │  │ HAS NOT GIVEN│
│  A WRITTEN   │  │ US A WRITTEN │
│  REVELATION  │  │  REVELATION  │
└──────────────┘  └──────────────┘
```

Someone might want to stop us at this point and express the possibility of a non-personal God which exists as a force rather than as a being. This viewpoint is represented by the box above on the right. A non-personal God could not give us a written revelation. Such a God in theory would be a force, but a force cannot be good or evil. A force is a thing not a being and can only be used in good or evil ways. So let's begin then by looking at the proposition that God does exist but has not given us a written revelation as a guide.

```
┌─────────────────────────┐
│    HAS NOT GIVEN US A   │
│    WRITTEN REVELATION   │
└─────────────────────────┘
```

CHAPTER ONE – GOD

If God exists and has not given us some revelation of Himself by which we can understand what He wants or expects from us, we are really not much better off than if He did not exist at all. We might be able to tell a little about Him by observing nature. We could probably discern that He is an orderly, creative and basically good God but not a great deal more. We might be able to discern a little more on the basis of conscience, but our consciences are not generally reliable guides and certainly cannot tell us about the nature of God. We would not know about an afterlife where we are judged. We would not understand the necessity or means of being saved. We would be on our own to figure out the meaning of life and to develop our own religion(s). This is actually the path that many today choose to take. They act like there is a God but do not want to believe that He has revealed His will for mankind.

But many of us believe that God *has* provided a revelation about Himself and spiritual matters of an eternal nature. However, even then there are vast differences. For example, some believe that God has revealed Himself in the Bible while others believe He has revealed Himself in other books as well. This takes us to the next level of our study.

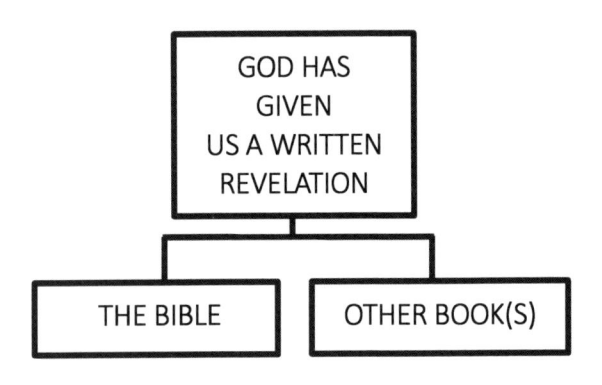

```
        ┌─────────────────┐
        │   GOD HAS       │
        │   GIVEN         │
        │   US A WRITTEN  │
        │   REVELATION    │
        └────────┬────────┘
         ┌──────┴──────┐
   ┌─────┴────┐   ┌────┴─────────┐
   │ THE BIBLE│   │OTHER BOOK(S) │
   └──────────┘   └──────────────┘
```

Let's begin by asking what it would be like if God had revealed Himself in a book or books other than the Bible. Maybe He has given *The Koran* to some people and *The Bhagavad Gita* to another group of people. Maybe *The Urantia Book* is a revelation as well as *Science and Health with the Key to Scriptures*. Since there are hundreds, if not thousands, of religions isn't it a little presumptuous of some people to say that *only* the Bible is the Word of God? If you

CHAPTER ONE – GOD

have to choose the right revelation(s) then you will have quite a job to discern which one(s) will serve your purposes. And since they each have their own angle you will probably end up with a religious stew. A little from this religion and a little from that. Of course, if you don't like a certain idea you can just choose another religion. One has to wonder what kind of God would reveal Himself in this way. Such a God would be a chameleon who refuses to be pinned down as to what is expected from people. If you choose the religion that satisfies you and allows you to live the way you want to live, you are really no better off than the person who does not believe that God exists at all. You are making up your own religion. It is "right" because you say it is right. You may even try and add the Bible in the mix. I have done this myself during my hippie years. I had a belief in the Eastern concept of God, the teaching of the Bible and a few other religions besides. You may not be confused, but I was! Of course, I didn't know just how confused I was.

FAITH WORKS

When a person believes that God has been revealed through books other than the Bible, they will soon discover many contradictory concepts of God. If all these other books agreed, then there would not need to be more than one book. You can have a religious stew but no continuity or compatibility because these other books conflict with each other.

Christians believe that God has only given us a written record of Himself in the Bible. Life becomes a bit simpler as we do not have to examine what other religions teach (although we may want to know a little about how they differ from the Bible so that we are not led astray). Since we believe the Bible is the only written revelation of God, our responsibility is much different. We cannot pick and choose what we like or dislike or believe or don't believe. We simply have to try and understand the teachings of the Bible and put them into practice. We read the Bible, ask God for understanding, and then apply it in our daily lives. This becomes a full time job. We will look a little closer at the importance and place of the Bible in the life of

CHAPTER ONE – GOD

a Christian in the next chapter. Hopefully by now you have decided where you are in your understanding of God.

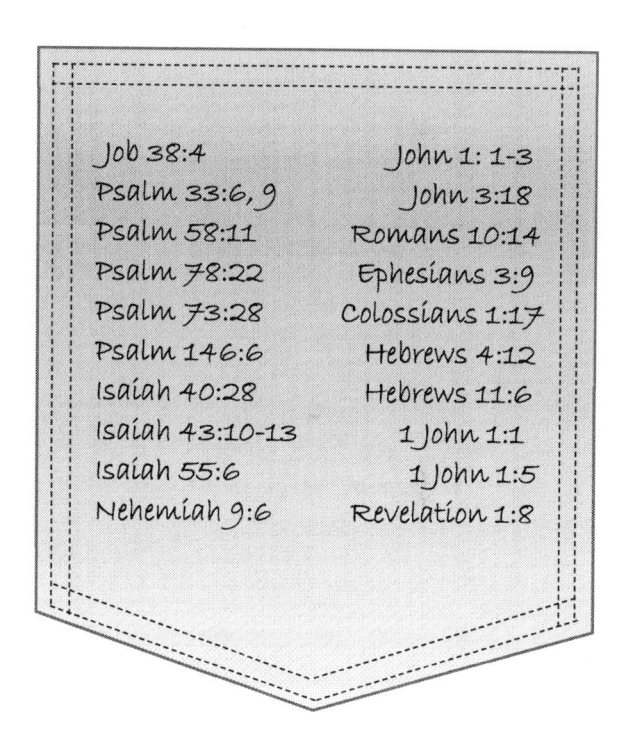

Job 38:4	John 1: 1-3
Psalm 33:6, 9	John 3:18
Psalm 58:11	Romans 10:14
Psalm 78:22	Ephesians 3:9
Psalm 73:28	Colossians 1:17
Psalm 146:6	Hebrews 4:12
Isaiah 40:28	Hebrews 11:6
Isaiah 43:10-13	1 John 1:1
Isaiah 55:6	1 John 1:5
Nehemiah 9:6	Revelation 1:8

FAITH WORKS

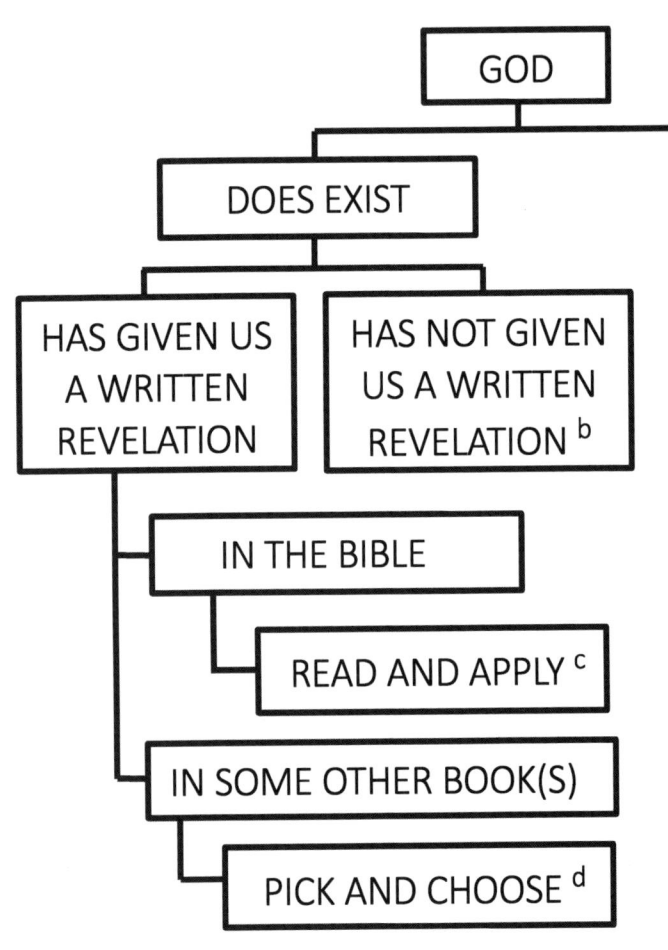

```
                    ┌──────────────┐
                    │     GOD      │
                    └──────┬───────┘
                           │
                    ┌──────┴───────┐
                    │  DOES EXIST  │
                    └──────┬───────┘
              ┌────────────┴────────────┐
        ┌─────────────┐           ┌──────────────┐
        │ HAS GIVEN US│           │ HAS NOT GIVEN│
        │  A WRITTEN  │           │  US A WRITTEN│
        │  REVELATION │           │ REVELATION [b]│
        └──────┬──────┘           └──────────────┘
               │
               ├──── IN THE BIBLE
               │         │
               │         └──── READ AND APPLY [c]
               │
               └──── IN SOME OTHER BOOK(S)
                         │
                         └──── PICK AND CHOOSE [d]
```

CHAPTER ONE – GOD

DOES NOT EXIST

NO DESIGN OR PURPOSE TO LIFE [a]

[a] No Judgment Day. No God to judge. No design or purpose.

[b] God is only revealed in nature and by subjective means. We are on our own to figure out the meaning of life.

[c] 1 Timothy 2:4, 5; Romans 1:17; Hebrews 11:6; Mark 12:29,30

[d] You can have a religious stew but no continuity or compatibility because other books conflict with each other.

FAITH WORKS

Q&A

Q. What happens to those who haven't heard about Jesus?

A. We can be sure that God is a just God and that He will never condemn anyone who does not deserve to be condemned.

People are condemned for rejecting God. The Bible tells us that all people know God exists. We also know that no one gets into heaven apart from the grace of God and the work of Christ on the cross. Usually this question is asked to dodge the real issue which is, "What will I do with the Jesus that I have heard about?"

Read the Word: Deuteronomy 29:29; Psalm 19:1-4; Matthew 7:7-11; John 14:6; Acts 4:12; Romans 1:19-20; Romans 2:15,16

Chapter Two

THE WORD OF GOD

In chapter one we tried to demonstrate not only that God exists but that He has revealed Himself in what we call the Holy Bible. How important is this? It is of unimaginable importance! We must have a revelation from God if we are to understand the meaning and purpose of life. We must have a revelation from God if we are to know how to live in this world. And we must have a revelation from God if we are to understand anything about life after death. Neither science nor philosophy can deal with these questions in a satisfactory way. Either we get the answer from God or we guess and grasp for answers.

The Bible tells us how mankind came into being and what God desires for our lives. It tells us how to live in a way that satisfies God, and it tells us how we can come to know God and spend eternity in His presence. It also tells us

FAITH WORKS

about our condition before God if we are not saved. It reveals that we either hate God or love Him (no matter what we may say). According to the Bible, if we reject God then we remain under His eternal wrath. While God loves us and expressed His love for us fully in Jesus, we are doomed to hell if we do not accept His Son's sacrifice in our behalf. Something of eternal significance has to take place in each of our lives if we want to spend eternity with God. The only alternative according to the Bible is to spend eternity apart from God.

The Bible is our sourcebook for information about spiritual matters, great and small. Of course the early Christians did not have the Bible as we do (but oh how they would have loved to). They were dependent upon the teachings of the Old Testament and the apostles. And they were utterly dependent upon the Holy Spirit to guide them into all truth.

We have an incredible privilege in having the completed Scriptures. We can read them, study them, mark them and memorize them. We

CHAPTER TWO – THE WORD OF GOD

have such an abundance of Bibles and so many translations available that we sometimes take them or granted. Many people do not even take them to church. Some people don't even know where their Bibles are. You will not make any real progress in your walk with God unless you give the Bible the recognition it deserves.

We are told that we are to desire the sincere milk of the Word. We are to drink in the teachings of the Bible like a newborn baby drinks milk. We ought to cry out if we can't seem to get a drink.

There are many fine versions of the Bible on the market today. I suggest reading from several translations and then selecting the one that speaks to your heart. Choose a few verses and compare them in each translation. Then compare a few passages such as some of the parables. Finally, try and read a short book from both the Old Testament and the New Testaments. You might even want to make a little comparison chart to record what you liked and

FAITH WORKS

did not like about each translation you are comparing.

I grew up with the King James Version so it has a special (but sentimental) place in my heart. I was introduced to the New International Version while at Bible college and used it as my primary Bible for many years, and when the New Living Translation was introduced in 1996, I fell in love with it. You may want to read passages in the New American Standard or the English Standard Version as well. Choose the Bible you will use.

I would suggest avoiding a so called "study Bible" in the beginning. While they do contain many helpful explanatory notes, they also often reflect an unnecessary bias that you want to avoid as much as possible. For the same reason I would shy away from a translation that is the work of one person as opposed to a group of translators. You can always upgrade to a study Bible after you have learned some of the basics of Christianity and sense the Lord's leading.

CHAPTER TWO – THE WORD OF GOD

For the Christian the Bible is the very voice of God. It is food for our souls and satisfies our spiritual thirst.

The object of our faith is Jesus Christ, but the source of our knowledge about Him is the Bible. Without the Bible we would be left to our own wonderings and wanderings. We believe it to be wholly true even though our understanding of it is at best incomplete. If the Bible is not true then life is an unsolvable mystery.

> What the pasture is
> to the herd,
> a house to a man,
> a nest to a bird,
> a stream to a fish,
> that the Bible is
> to faithful souls.
> Martin Luther

FAITH WORKS

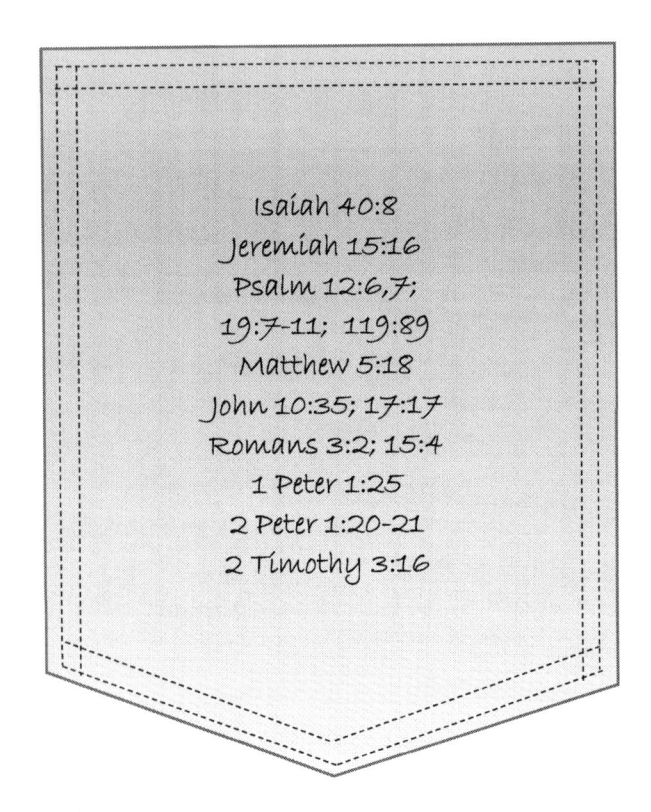

Isaiah 40:8
Jeremiah 15:16
Psalm 12:6,7;
19:7-11; 119:89
Matthew 5:18
John 10:35; 17:17
Romans 3:2; 15:4
1 Peter 1:25
2 Peter 1:20-21
2 Timothy 3:16

Chapter Three

THE SON OF GOD

From His miraculous conception (Who has ever heard of a virgin having a child?) to His resurrection from the dead (Who has ever heard of someone raising his or her self from the dead?), the life of Jesus is the focus of the Bible. The Old Testament leads up to, expects and reveals the future coming of a Savior. The New Testament reveals the Savior who came and shows how He fulfilled the Old Testament.

> *God can do what He chooses within the bounds of His self-imposed limits.*

The Bible presents Jesus as more than a teacher, more than an example, more than a hero, even more than a revolutionary; it presents Jesus as God Himself. While this is difficult to understand, so is the very concept of

FAITH WORKS

God. God chose to become a human being. Man cannot become God, but God could become a man. Since Jesus was God in the flesh He was able to live a sinless life; in fact, it can be argued that since He was God He could not sin. Jesus lived a perfect life, taught perfect ways and died so that we could come into a right relationship with God.

This is why Christians worship Jesus and Jesus alone. We believe the Bible clearly teaches that He is God. We cannot understand how God can be the Father, the Son and the Spirit all at the same time, but the Bible does clearly teach us that this is true. One day we will understand.

We believe that Jesus died in our place so that we could be brought into a right relationship with God. We believe that when we accept Him into our lives, God the Holy Spirit actually enters our lives and gives us the ability to follow God from that moment forward. We believe that after Jesus died He was raised from the dead, met with disciples and then He was taken back home to heaven. We believe that even

CHAPTER THREE – THE SON OF GOD

now He is at work praying for us, preparing a place for us, planning a celebration for us and that He will soon return for us!

A few facts about Jesus:

He is the Creator and Sustainer of all life.
John 1:1-3; Colossians 1:16, 17

He is the visible image of the invisible God.
John 14:9; Colossians 1:15

He lived a sinless life and died for our sins.
2 Corinthians 5:21; Revelation 1:5

He is alive in heaven and working for us.
Romans 8:34; Colossians 3:1

He will come back for His followers and take us to be with Him.
John 14:3; Hebrews 9:28

FAITH WORKS

Q&A

Q. Is Jesus the only way to get to know God?

A. Yes, because Jesus is God. He rebuked those people who claimed to know and love God but rejected Him. He could do this because He is God. If Jesus were less than God then other religions might be acceptable. Since God Himself became a man and lived a perfect life and died for us to live with Him He decides who gets to know Him. The Bible is very clear that there is no other way to be saved.

Read the Word: John 8:24; 10:7; 14:6; Acts 4:12; 1 Corinthians 8:6; 1 Timothy 2:5; Hebrews 2:3 1 John 2:23; 5:12

Chapter Four

THE SPIRIT OF GOD

Before Jesus left the earth to return to heaven, He promised His followers that He would not leave them behind as orphans. He was incredibly concerned about His followers. He told them, and us through them, that He would send us a Helper. This Helper is not just so we can survive, but so we can flourish as His children even though we no longer have His physical presence.

The Holy Spirit lives inside each person who truly accepts Jesus as their Lord and Savior. The Bible clearly teaches that if we do not have the Holy Spirit living in us, we are not Christians (Romans 8:9).

The Holy Spirit does several things. First, He convicts people that they are sinners in need of

FAITH WORKS

a Savior. Not everyone responds to this conviction by repenting and accepting Christ, but some do. As Christians we also are often convicted when we sin, and this is without question the work of the Spirit of God in us. But the Bible speaks of the convicting work of the Spirit as something that happens prior to salvation (John 16:8). When He convicts us He is calling us to repent and ask for salvation. When we do this we are *born again*, and the Holy Spirit comes into our lives and gives us the resources we need to walk with God.

While we may not be able to describe the Holy Spirit in a satisfying manner, we know that when He enters our lives He transforms them! We are not concerned with the shape or form of the Spirit, but we should be concerned that we are allowing Him to work in our lives.

The Holy Spirit is regarded as God just as the Father is God and Jesus is God. This means that He deserves the same worship and honor that we give to Jesus.

CHAPTER FOUR – THE SPIRIT OF GOD

A few facts about the Holy Spirit:

He is revealed as being God.
Acts 5:3, 4; Hebrews 3:7-11

He lives inside Christians.
1 Corinthians 6:19; 1 John 3:24

He guides us into all truth.
John 14:26; 1 John 2:27

He empowers us to lead godly lives.
1 Peter 1:5; 2 Peter 1:3

He comforts us when we suffer.
Romans 8:26, 27; 2 Corinthians 1:4

FAITH WORKS

Q&A

Q. Why do people suffer?

A. People suffer because of sin. Satan is the author of sin and sin affects all people. Even the innocent suffer as a result of the sin of Adam and Eve. While there are many *reasons* for suffering (and suffering can be used for our own good), the ultimate *cause* of suffering is the fall of mankind. What is different for us as Christians is that we look forward to a future where there will be no more sin or suffering. One thing we should all consider is how much Jesus Himself, the sinless One, suffered in our behalf!

Read the Word: Genesis 3:17-19; Job 1; John 9:3; Acts 17:3; 2 Corinthians 5:21; Hebrews 13:12; 1 Peter 3:18; Revelation 21:4

Chapter Five

The Children of God

Those of us who have been born again are called children of God. While the world around us might ignore our status and ridicule us, one day they will envy us.

As God's children we have God as our Father. He has adopted us into His family. We are to look to Him for spiritual nourishment. He has given us new hearts and new minds. We have a new King (Jesus) and we are promised new bodies and a new kingdom!

As God's children we have a new family. We are brothers and sisters in Christ. We have a bond that is deeper and more meaningful than that of our biological families. This bond actually deepens our love and concern for our "earthly" families as well. The Christian faith teaches us that we are to care for our families as well as our family in Christ. Jesus regards us as His

FAITH WORKS

brothers and sisters as well. You will be interested to know how we are to live as the family of God, so as you read your New Testament pay special attention to that little phrase "one another."

While the only way a person can become a Christian is by accepting Christ, not everyone comes to Christ for the same reason. Some accept Christ because they know their lives are empty and meaningless apart from Him. They are at the end of their ropes and know they need change. Some people come to Christ because they know that one day they will die and want to go to heaven after they die. Some people simply know they need Christ because they are sinners and need salvation. There are many reasons people come to Christ to be saved. Whatever your reason for coming to Christ, you need to know that He will change your life. If you think your life doesn't need changing, then you probably have never really dealt with the effects of sin in your life.

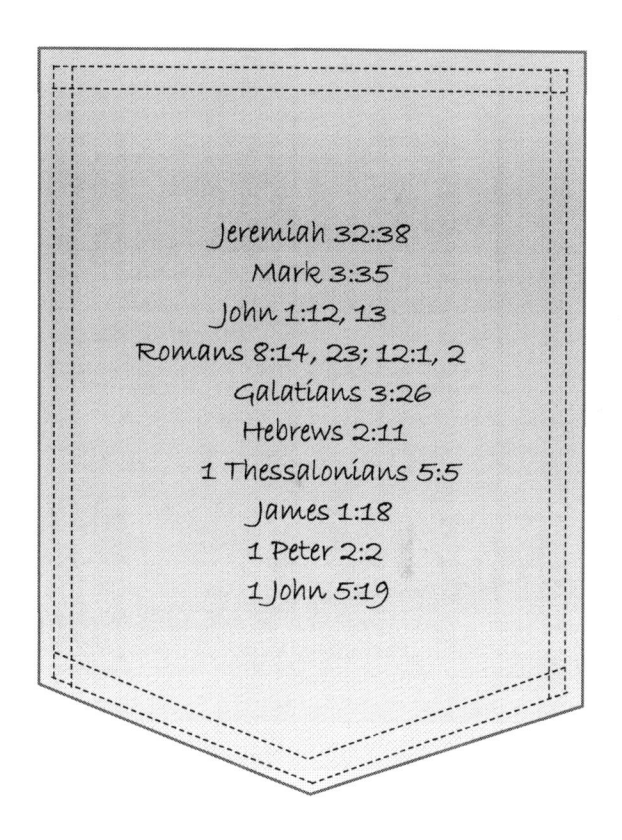

CHAPTER FIVE – THE CHILDREN OF GOD

Jeremiah 32:38
Mark 3:35
John 1:12, 13
Romans 8:14, 23; 12:1, 2
Galatians 3:26
Hebrews 2:11
1 Thessalonians 5:5
James 1:18
1 Peter 2:2
1 John 5:19

FAITH WORKS

Why not take a moment to "Examine yourself and be sure that you are in the faith." (2 Corinthians 13:5)

How to Let God Find You

Admit to God that you are a sinner and that your sin has separated you from Him.

"For all have sinned; and fall short of God's glorious standard." Romans 3:23

"For the wages of sin is death, but the free gift of God is eternal life through Christ Jesus our Lord." Romans 6:23

Believe that God exists and that He wants to save you.

"Anyone who wants to come to Him must believe that there is a God and that He rewards those who earnestly seek Him." Hebrews 11:6

"He (God) wants everyone to be saved and to understand the truth." 1 Timothy 2:4

CHAPTER FIVE – THE CHILDREN OF GOD

Confess that Jesus is the One who died for your sins.

"For if you confess with your mouth that Jesus is Lord and believe in your heart that God raised Him from the dead, you will be saved. For it is by believing in your heart that you are made right with God, and it is by confessing with your mouth that you are saved." Romans 10:9, 10

Demonstrate your faith in God by following Jesus Christ from now on.

"So our aim is to please Him always." 2 Corinthians 5:9

"Try to find out what is pleasing to the Lord." Ephesians 5:10

FAITH WORKS

notes

Part Two

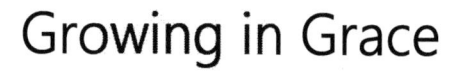

Growing in Grace

He is no fool who gives what he cannot keep
to gain what he cannot lose.
Jim Elliot

If you try to keep your life for yourself you will lose it, but if you give up your life for me you will gain it. Luke 9:24

If anyone acknowledges me publicly before men I will openly acknowledge that person before my Father in heaven.
Matthew 10:32

In this section we will look at what it means to grow in grace. How do we make progress in our walk with God?

This is an area that is largely ignored by many Christians, and as a result they make little or no headway in their spiritual lives.

2 Corinthians 5:9 says that as followers of God *we are to make it our goal to please Him.* How can we do this unless we discover what pleases Him by reading the Bible, the source of spiritual truth? Ephesians 5:10 tells *us to find out what pleases the Lord.* We find out what pleases God by reading and listening to His word.

My personal discipleship plan has been about as simple as possible. God shows me what to do and I try and do it! I call it the two-step process. I often fall short but I still think it is the easiest and best plan in our busy society.

When I started walking with God seriously, I was living on a commune in Vermont. God showed me clearly that if I were to follow Him I

FAITH WORKS

had to stop using drugs (Romans 13:1, 2). By His grace, and only by His grace, I stopped right then and there. Next, He showed me that I had to leave the commune where I was living. His word was as clear to me as if He had spoken audibly (2 Corinthians 6:14-17). This was not easy to do as these were "my people" and this was "my home." But the only choice I had was to obey or disobey. Next I asked God what I was supposed to do when I left. Once again the answer came from the Bible; get a job and repay your debts (Ephesians 4:28). Simple? Well, yes, but impossible without the grace of God.

The following chapters in this section are based on 2 Peter 1:5-7 and reveal a pattern that we can use to help our faith grow. Whether this was a pattern that was observed by Peter, or if he felt this was a proper way for believers to grow, we cannot be sure. Perhaps it is both. Regardless, I cannot help but see a pattern here that can help us to grow in our understanding and application of faith.

PART TWO – GROWING IN GRACE

For this very reason, make every effort to add to your faith goodness; and to goodness, knowledge; and to knowledge, self-control; and to self-control, perseverance; and to perseverance, godliness; and to godliness, brotherly kindness; and to brotherly kindness, love.
2 Peter 1:5-7 NIV

FAITH WORKS

Q&A

Q. How can miracles be possible?

A. If God exists then miracles do not present a difficulty. When Jesus walked the earth He performed many miracles because He was God. The miracles that Jesus did were to show people that the things He taught were from God.

Read the Word: Genesis 18:14; Numbers 11:23; 1 Samuel 14:6; 2 Kings 7:2; Job 42:2; Jeremiah 32:17; Zechariah 8:6; Matthew 3:9; Matthew 19:26; Ephesians 3:20; Hebrews 11:19

Chapter Six

Add to Your Faith...

Our faith is more than a word. It is an actual possession; it is a thing, even if it is not something we can see with our eyes, touch with our hands, smell with our noses or taste with our tongues. We know when we have it, and it is fairly obvious when we don't. James tells us that unless faith is accompanied by works, it is not really faith. It is useless. It is dead. Our faith must bear fruit.

What is faith? Faith is believing in the promises of God. We believe whatever God has promised. We believe we will be saved if we accept Christ. We believe the lost will be damned because that is a promise of God.

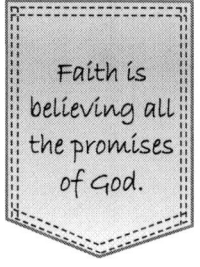

> Faith is believing all the promises of God.

FAITH WORKS

Faith is believing God. Trusting Him. When we really trust Him then we want to please Him. Why would we ever want to do anything that does not please the One who sacrificed so much to save us?

We read that Abraham was accepted because he believed God. He looked forward to the coming of God's kingdom. He put his faith in God, and as a result God considered him "righteous." That is, God accepted him as a friend. We are either friends of God or enemies, and there is no in between. There is no fence sitting when it comes to salvation.

Acts 15:9   Romans 3:22-30

2 Corinthians 4:18; 13:5

Galatians 2:16; 5:6

Ephesians 2:8,9; 6:16

Colossians 2:7

1 Timothy 1:19; 6:12

Hebrews 11:1   James 2:18;

1 Peter 1:7,8

Chapter Seven

Goodness

Peter places goodness as the next quality to be added. Perhaps this is because we do not have to know a whole lot in order to begin doing good deeds. Good deeds should be one of the first expressions of our new found faith because our lives have been transformed. We may have done many good things before we accepted Christ, but now our lives are to be full of good deeds. In fact, we discover that we were saved to do good works. Even more mysteriously, we were saved to do the good works that God planned for us to do from before the creation of the world.

James tells us that if our faith does not produce good deeds, it is a useless faith. Hebrews tells us that we are to be actively thinking of ways to motivate others to perform good deeds. Good deeds are the first evidences that our faith is genuine. Just as our faith is something

FAITH WORKS

that is to last throughout the rest of our lives, we are to continue doing good deeds for the rest of our journey as well. These good deeds are products of faith, not the source of faith. Some people think they will get to heaven by their good deeds, but God does not save people on the basis of good deeds. He only saves us on the basis of faith.

This goodness is not to be defined strictly as deeds being done. It includes the thoughts that we think and the words that we speak. It is a new person being formed in an old body. We speak things that help people, and we think about things that please God. It is a goodness that pours forth from us as a result of what God has done for us. Of course we will continue to struggle and our selfish nature will tempt us to do wrong, but overall our lives will be changing for good.

Perhaps part of the reason Peter puts good deeds ahead of knowledge is that we are tempted to talk about what we know before people see any change in the way we live.

CHAPTER SEVEN – GOODNESS

Someone said, "People don't care how much you know until they know how much you care!"

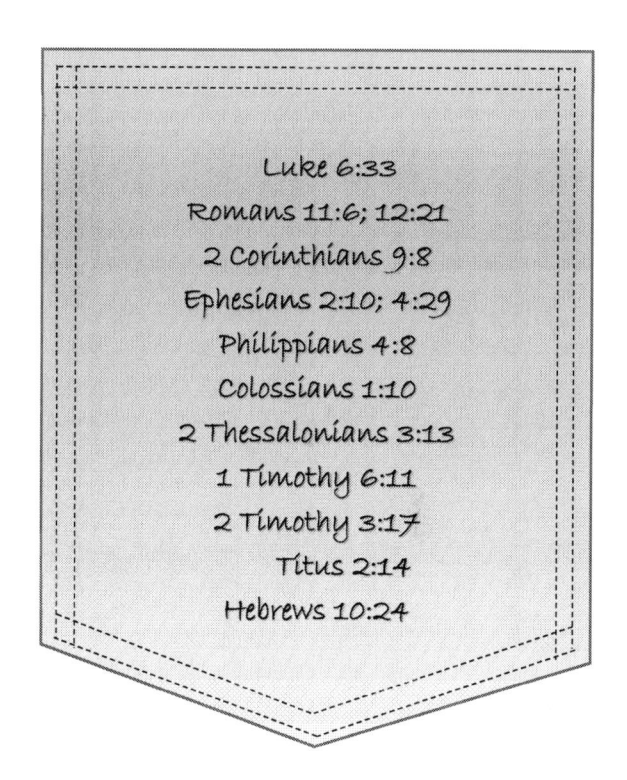

Luke 6:33

Romans 11:6; 12:21

2 Corinthians 9:8

Ephesians 2:10; 4:29

Philippians 4:8

Colossians 1:10

2 Thessalonians 3:13

1 Timothy 6:11

2 Timothy 3:17

Titus 2:14

Hebrews 10:24

FAITH WORKS

Q&A

Q. Does the Bible have errors in it?

A. The errors that people often point out are not errors like mistakes but things that *seem* to contradict each other. There are many things in the Bible that are difficult to understand or reconcile in our minds. The problem is that we see truths that *appear* to conflict with each other. We need to always remember that the Bible is not a book of logistical truth so much as it is a revelation of spiritual truth. One day we will understand the things that trouble our thinking now. It is important to remember that these so called *errors* do not affect the things we believe or the way we are to behave.

Read the Word: Deuteronomy 29:29; Job 11:7; Proverbs 25:2; Ecclesiastes 8:17; Isaiah 8:20; Romans 11:33, 34; 1 Corinthians 13:9

Chapter Eight

Knowledge

As we grow in our faith by doing good works, we should also be learning more about our faith. We call this *growing in knowledge*. We want to know more about God, more about the Bible, more about how we are to live as believers, and many other things.

The Bible tells us that when we first come to Christ we are like babies, and we should want God to feed us as a mother feeds her babies (1 Peter 2:2). We need and desire the basic simple truths of the Bible. Once we get the basics down, we can begin to comprehend the deeper truths of the Bible. For now focus on what is clear and easy to understand. Don't try to hurry the process or get caught up in things that might stunt your growth. Avoid listening to people who simply want you to believe the way they do on issues that you do not under-

FAITH WORKS

stand. Focus on things like what you should believe about Jesus, the church and the way you should be living out your faith. God will show you when you are ready to grasp deeper truths. The book that you are reading now is what God wants you to be reading because it is not deep or profound, but it is simple and directs you right back to Him and His word.

This growing in knowledge is so important that those who refuse to learn more shrivel in the faith. You do not have to be a great reader or student, but you do have to set aside a time for learning more of the Bible's teaching. Maybe you cannot read but you can listen. You can learn if you want to, and if you don't want to learn then you need to ask yourself why. Why don't you want to know more about God? Why don't you want to know about how to live as a Christian?

A knowledge of God can only be gained by reading the Bible. To refuse to read the Bible is refusing to hear the voice of God. God's children want to hear the voice of God. It is the

CHAPTER EIGHT – KNOWLEDGE

voice of our Father calling us, comforting us, gently training us and guiding us on the path to heaven.

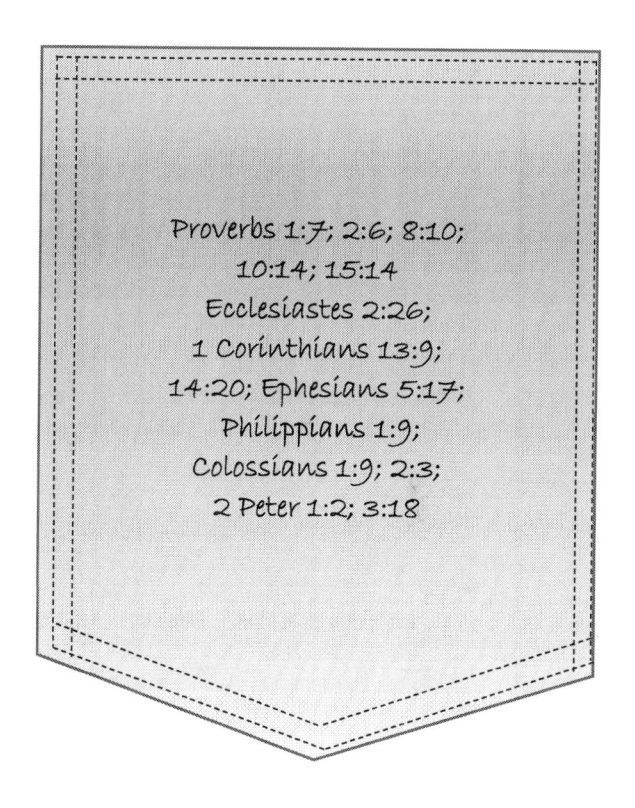

> Proverbs 1:7; 2:6; 8:10;
> 10:14; 15:14
> Ecclesiastes 2:26;
> 1 Corinthians 13:9;
> 14:20; Ephesians 5:17;
> Philippians 1:9;
> Colossians 1:9; 2:3;
> 2 Peter 1:2; 3:18

FAITH WORKS

Q&A

Q. Isn't being a Christian just a change of mentality?

A. This is one of the biggest problems we face as Christians. People come to church and try to act like Christians without being born again. There is no easy way to explain this but: *Christianity is an experience not an experiment.*

Read the Word: Romans 8:11; Ephesians 2:6; Titus 3:5; 1 Peter 1:3, 23; 4:4

Chapter Nine

Self-Control

This step is a little harder than the previous ones. It is not real hard to do good deeds. It is not terribly difficult to read the Bible and get knowledge. But to actually do what the Bible says can be a little harder. To respond to an unkind person with kindness, for example takes an act of the will. This act of the will is self-control.

Self-control is listed as a fruit or a product of the Holy Spirit in Galatians 5:23. Self-control is the ability that God endows us with to follow His instructions and do His will. He doesn't just tell us to live a certain lifestyle, but He gives us the ability to live it as well. Doing what God wants is not always easy, in fact it can be painful at times. But doing His will is always the right thing to do, and it is what He expects us to do.

FAITH WORKS

For example, when I first started walking with God I had a problem with swearing. I had developed a very foul tongue over the years, and while I knew it was wrong, I also felt powerless to stop. I confessed this problem to a brother in Christ and he quoted Ephesians 4:29 to me. Hearing what God said about foul language gave me a stronger desire to stop swearing. That desire, along with the Holy Spirit now living in me, gave me all I needed to overcome the problem of swearing. I am still far from perfect, but my language is a lot better!

Of course we all have many areas we need to be working on as we develop self-control. At the same time I was struggling with my swearing I was still smoking. By the grace of God I was able to stop smoking and swearing at the same period of my life.

Even after over 35 years I still struggle with self-control in other areas. God knows we will not be perfect in this lifetime, but He does expect us to try and make progress. Self-control is God empowered will power. It is acknowledging

CHAPTER NINE – SELF CONTROL

that I cannot do it on my own, but I can do it with God's help.

Walking with Jesus demands that we choose the right path and stay on the right path. Of course He will find us if we stray, but we are not to test the grace of God.

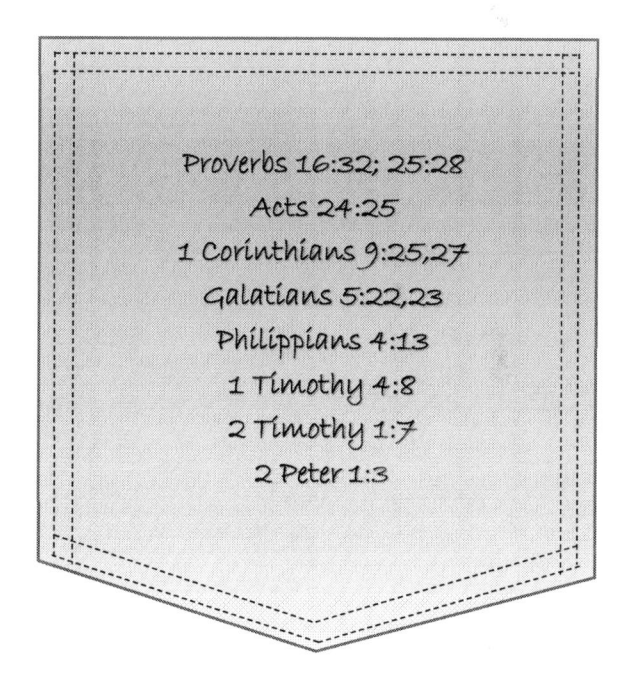

> Proverbs 16:32; 25:28
> Acts 24:25
> 1 Corinthians 9:25,27
> Galatians 5:22,23
> Philippians 4:13
> 1 Timothy 4:8
> 2 Timothy 1:7
> 2 Peter 1:3

FAITH WORKS

Q&A

Q. Won't I go to heaven if I live a good clean life?

A. You cannot live a good clean life. God and heaven are absolutely pure and perfect and only those who have been made clean by the blood of Jesus are allowed into heaven. As a little test just read through the Ten Commandments to see if you have always obeyed each of them perfectly.

Read the Word: 1 Kings 8:46; Job 14:4; 15:14; Psalm 51:5; Proverbs 20:9; Ecclesiastes 7:20 Romans 3:23; Galatians 3:22; James 3:2; 1 John 1:10

Chapter Ten

Perseverance

Many people make a good start in the Christian life but they do not persevere. They stop. They give up. They give in to peer pressure, whether it is to their friends, the media or to society as a whole. Someone said, "Christianity has not been tried and found wanting but it has been found difficult and left untried!"

Jesus warned it would be this way for many people in His parable about the good seed in Matthew 13:3-8. Later, in verses 18-23, He explained that there were three basic reasons people didn't continue in the faith after professing to be His followers. In verse 19 the seed was planted in the head but didn't take root in the heart. It sounded good at first, but when Satan caused them to see all the things they would miss, they said, "Forget it," and turned their backs on Christ.

FAITH WORKS

In verses 20-21 another type of person accepted the word as well. They believed it but were not willing to live it out. When living for Christ became difficult they abandoned Him. They did not want to be ridiculed or persecuted for their faith, and so they gave up. Jesus declared their faith was worthless.

A third group of people in verse 22 would not follow Christ because the pull of the world was too strong. They wanted the things this world had to offer more than they wanted to follow Christ.

In light of this we each need to heed the call of Jesus to follow Him. We need to hear what He says and do it. If we refuse to obey Him we can hardly call ourselves His followers. Jesus did not say we would be happy if we just heard His words. He said we would be happy if we do what He says (John 13:17).

Jesus warned people to count the cost of following Him. His is no easy path of discipleship. But He promised to help us (Matthew 11:28-30).

CHAPTER TEN – PERSEVERANCE

Winston Churchill once gave a very short speech at a boy's academy graduation ceremony. It was just nine short, but probably never forgotten words, "Never give up. Never give up. Never give up." That is the idea of perseverance: never give up. Go forwards, not backwards!

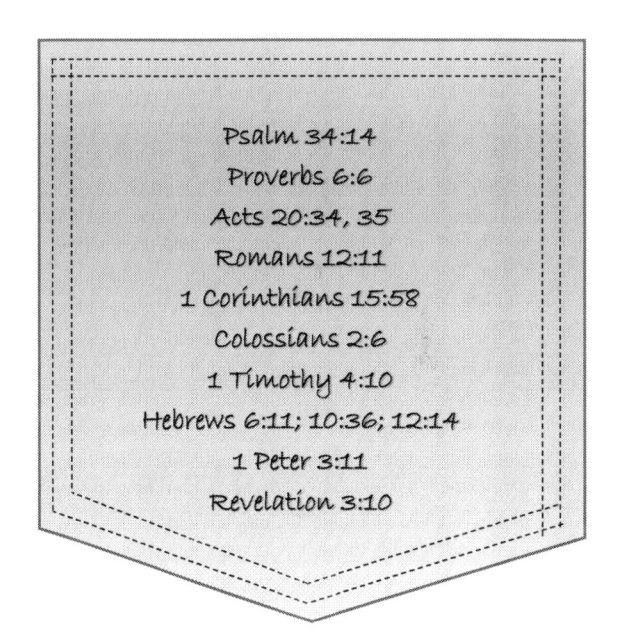

Psalm 34:14

Proverbs 6:6

Acts 20:34, 35

Romans 12:11

1 Corinthians 15:58

Colossians 2:6

1 Timothy 4:10

Hebrews 6:11; 10:36; 12:14

1 Peter 3:11

Revelation 3:10

FAITH WORKS

notes

Chapter Eleven

Godliness

What in the world does godliness mean? It means that we live the way God desires us to live. It means living our lives with reverence for God. Sometimes we gain a better understanding of a word by considering what the opposite word means. Ungodliness would be living in ways that displease God. It can even result in His anger or wrath. Godliness then is living in a manner that pleases God. It is acting like a child of God.

The Bible commends godly living, and the New Testament is very clear that as Christians we are to live in a Christ like way. This does not mean that we walk around healing the sick and raising the dead or turning water into wine. It means that we think wholesome thoughts, do good deeds and speak words that show that we have been born again, that we are children of God. We are children of the light and we are to walk in the light. This means that we have

FAITH WORKS

nothing to hide. We live in such a way that everything we think, say or do brings honor and glory to God. That is godly living. Part of godly living is understanding that we are not really very godly! Part of godly living is remembering to confess our sins and asking God to give us the desire to abandon them as well (1 John 1:9).

Of course we do not walk around thinking of ourselves as godly any more than the ungodly think of themselves as ungodly. If others call us godly, then we are humbly blessed but should not boast. Instead, we should thank God that someone sees our spiritual growth. Godliness is a goal to be aimed for and a quality to be desired.

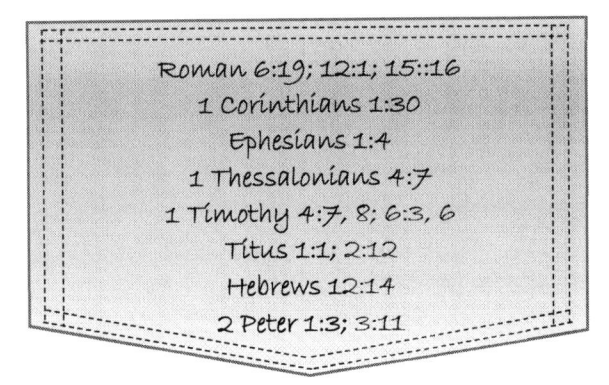

Roman 6:19; 12:1; 15::16
1 Corinthians 1:30
Ephesians 1:4
1 Thessalonians 4:7
1 Timothy 4:7, 8; 6:3, 6
Titus 1:1; 2:12
Hebrews 12:14
2 Peter 1:3; 3:11

Chapter Twelve

Brotherly Kindness

The book of 1 John tells us that one of the evidences that we have been born again is that we love our Christian brothers and sisters. Jesus Himself told us that people would know we are His followers because of the love we have for each other.

While brotherly kindness may not be a term that is easily defined, it is something we know when we see it. There is a tender affection evident in the lives of Christians because we have the same Father. We are a family. A family that knows no borders. We are one with our brothers and sisters in Christ even if they don't speak our language or share our culture. We have a family bond because of a spiritual experience.

According to 1 Timothy we are to treat older men and women as fathers and mothers and

FAITH WORKS

younger men and women as brothers and sisters.

This is a beautiful picture of how we ought to treat each other in God's kingdom based on how family relationships should be on earth. If our family relationships have not been as they ought to be, we can see from the New Testament how we should regard our biological families as well as our spiritual family.

There is normally a natural affection for our family members even when we disagree. We still love and care for each other and want to protect, provide for and honor our family. In our spiritual family we want to correct our brothers and sisters if we see them heading the wrong way, and we want to restore them if they have made mistakes. We gladly teach and help them, are concerned about them and yes, at times we simply have to put up with them!

As you read through the New Testament take special notice of how we are to treat each other

CHAPTER TWELVE – BROTHERLY KINDNESS

as children of God. You will be surprised at how much instruction we are given.

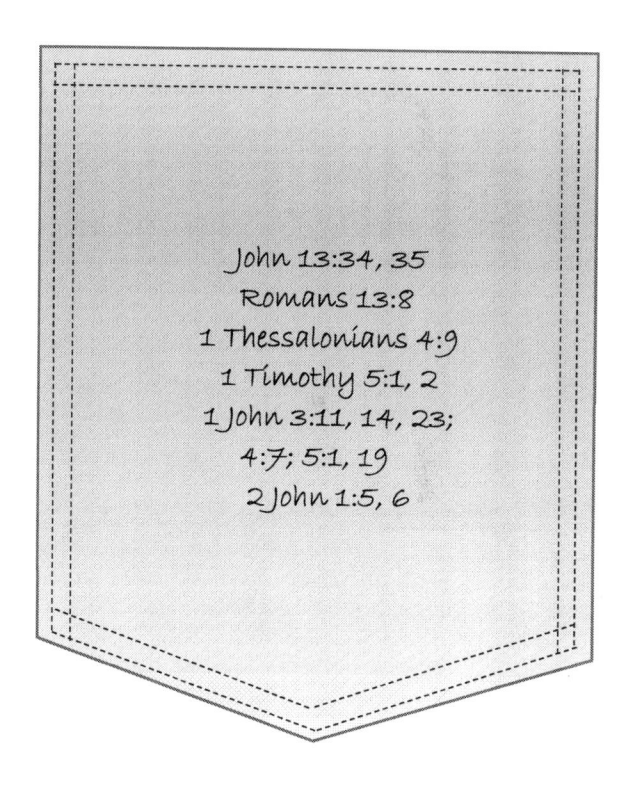

> John 13:34, 35
> Romans 13:8
> 1 Thessalonians 4:9
> 1 Timothy 5:1, 2
> 1 John 3:11, 14, 23;
> 4:7; 5:1, 19
> 2 John 1:5, 6

FAITH WORKS

notes

Chapter Thirteen

Love

Of course, love is the overarching reason for everything we do. We read that God is love. This does not mean that God is an inanimate force or energy. It means that love is the very best way to describe God. Everything God does is an expression of His love in one way or another. The highest expression of God's love was sending Jesus to die for our sins.

People should know we are Christians by our love for one another. This is not the love of the counterculture movement of the 60's, but the love of God's counterculture. To love others means to care about them. God showed how much He cared for us by dying for us. We are supposed to care for others as a result of His love in us.

When we don't care about others we are not acting as God would have us to. To not care is

FAITH WORKS

to not love and to disgrace God. God has given us new life, and we should wonder if we have received this new life if there is anyone that we do not care about. We should care about the person on the street, our co-workers, our President and everyone else as well. Of course we will not agree with everyone, but that does not mean we don't care about them. This is one reason we do not ignore people or their needs.

Hatred for a person is often expressed by simply ignoring that person. Perhaps the saddest thing of all is that this is how people express their hatred of God: they simply ignore Him and treat Him as if He does not exist.

God showed His love for us by sending His Son to die for us. We show our love for God by doing what He tells us to do. One of the things He clearly tells us to do is love each other.

CHAPTER THIRTEEN – LOVE

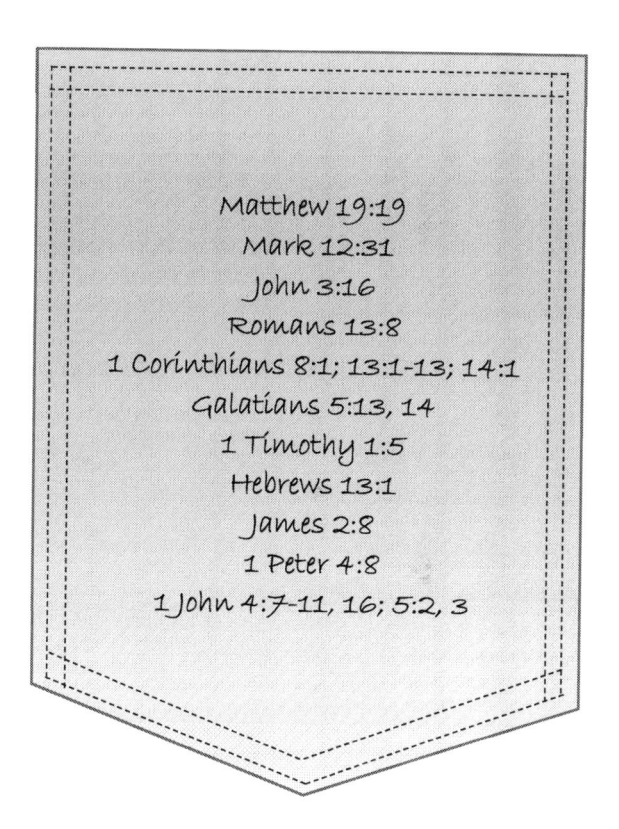

Matthew 19:19
Mark 12:31
John 3:16
Romans 13:8
1 Corinthians 8:1; 13:1-13; 14:1
Galatians 5:13, 14
1 Timothy 1:5
Hebrews 13:1
James 2:8
1 Peter 4:8
1 John 4:7-11, 16; 5:2, 3

FAITH WORKS

notes

Chapter Fourteen

The Reason

For if you possess these qualities in increasing measure, they will keep you from being ineffective and unproductive in your knowledge of our Lord Jesus Christ.
2 Peter 1:8

If you want to be the person God designed you to be, then the qualities we have been looking at in this section are essential to your goal. As you develop these qualities you will produce a life that pleases God, and in so doing, you will find a satisfaction that exceeds anything you have ever experienced.

We cannot pick and choose the qualities listed in 2 Peter and simply focus on the ones we think will be easy or that we want to develop. All of these qualities (and many others as well) need to be developed. They are like the strands in a rope. Each strand is important.

FAITH WORKS

God wants to see us grow in our faith and is pleased when we live in ways that honor Him. He is like a parent who takes a great deal of pleasure in a newborn baby but also wants to see us grow into spiritually mature people.

God understands very well at what stage of growth we are, and He makes every provision to see us reach the next level. We want to use those provisions wisely, whether they are books, teachers, or the incredible work of the Holy Spirit in our lives. The New Testament clearly teaches us that we are to "make every effort." (Luke 13:24; 2 Peter 1:5, 3:14)

Part Three

Other Matters

FAITH WORKS

In the play *The King and I*, the king often uses the phrase, "Etcetera, etcetera, etcetera." In God's world the etcetera's are not unnecessary additions but more things that we must take into account. The following information is what I would have liked to have at my fingertips when I first started walking with God. This information is only the beginning point, and you will find that when you walk with God, He will be constantly giving you some new area to be considering as you grow in the faith you have embraced.

As Jesus said, "Now that you know these things, happy are you if you do them!"
John 13:17

Chapter Fifteen

Prayer

Prayer often sounds dull and dry, and for that reason I hesitate to put it first. But it is first. You cannot be saved if you do not pray. Your very first act as a Christian is to talk to God and ask Him to save you. You will never experience the growth that God wants for you to have unless you learn to spend time with Him. This is a privilege to be embraced because you and I can enter into the very presence of the Creator of the universe, and He will listen to us as if we were the only person in the universe!

Prayer is communicating with God. We communicate with each other in many ways in our age. We can simply talk to each other, text, type, Skype, or even write letters. The important thing in communicating is that the one on the receiving end understands what you are saying. Our prayer life is much like this. The important thing is that God understands what you

FAITH WORKS

are saying. Of course God knows everything already so many people think that prayer is not necessary. But we cannot read through the Scriptures without seeing how important prayer is. To neglect prayer is to neglect God. It is like having a friend that you never call, write or talk to; such a friend would be unnecessary.

It is important to set aside special time(s) for prayer. Jesus taught us to pray every day. The Bible tells us we are always to be praying. If we do not set aside a special time and place for prayer, we will probably find ourselves praying less and less *and* enjoying it less and less. As we grow in our faith, we should find that we are praying more and more and enjoying it more and more. Prayer is having intimate communion with God Himself. Until we understand this, prayer is likely to be a burden rather than a privilege. Some people ignore prayer, claiming that their entire lives are devoted to God. But we should all have devoted lives, and part of that devotion should be private prayers. Do not

CHAPTER FIFTEEN – PRAYER

deprive yourself of the deep pleasure of knowing God. Only by knowing Him will you be able to truly make progress in your faith.

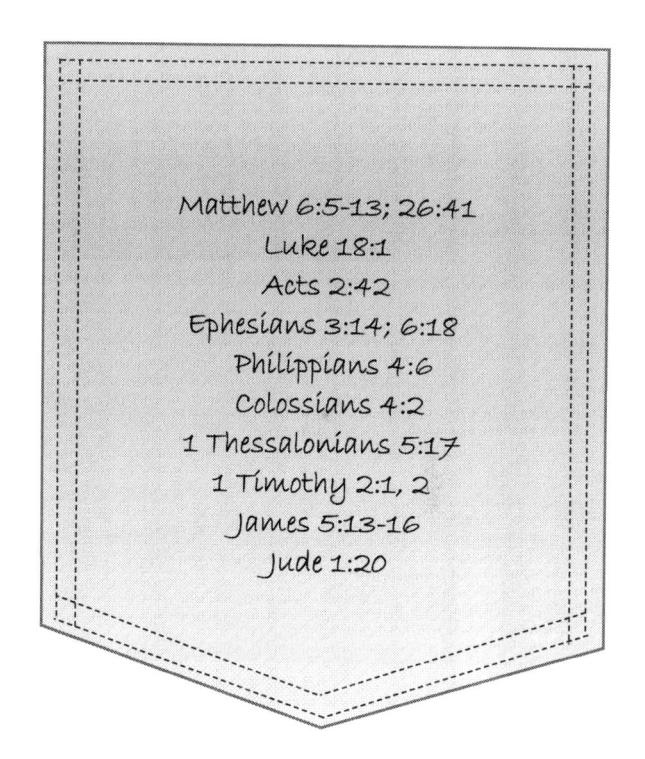

> Matthew 6:5-13; 26:41
> Luke 18:1
> Acts 2:42
> Ephesians 3:14; 6:18
> Philippians 4:6
> Colossians 4:2
> 1 Thessalonians 5:17
> 1 Timothy 2:1, 2
> James 5:13-16
> Jude 1:20

FAITH WORKS

notes

Chapter Sixteen

Bible Reading

While prayer allows us to communicate with God, Bible reading allows God to communicate with us. We tell Him what our desires are by praying, and He tells us what His desires are as we read His word. How will we ever know what He wants if we don't read His word on a regular basis?

There are many Bible reading plans available, but the best plan is the one that you will use. A person should read some of the Old Testament and some of the New Testament each day. The Old Testament predicts the coming of Jesus and the New Testament presents the coming of Jesus. While there are no rules, I would try to read at least a chapter of the Old Testament and a chapter of the New Testament every day. Don't get caught up in reading a certain amount if you are not understanding what you read. Read less if you need to in order to get

FAITH WORKS

more out of it. There will be some places where you may just have to plow through without much understanding. For example, books like Leviticus and Revelation do not easily yield their secrets.

I use what might be called a modified Mc Cheyne plan. This plan involves reading two chapters of the Old Testament and two of the New Testament each day. I read from Genesis through 2nd Chronicles and from Ezra through Malachi. I also read a chapter from the Gospels each day and then a chapter from Acts through Revelation. I have found this to be a good pattern for me. You can develop and follow your own plan.

In chapter 2 we talked about Bibles and how to choose a Bible to use. You may want to reread that chapter at this point.

The Word of God is so thrilling and fulfilling that we should be wearing out our Bibles as we use them!

CHAPTER SIXTEEN – BIBLE READING

Deuteronomy 17:19
Joshua 1:8
Psalm 1:1-3
Psalm 119
Matthew 4:4
Luke 8:15; 11:28
Acts 6:4; 17:11
2 Corinthians 2:17; 4:2
Hebrews 4:12
James 1:22
2 Timothy 2:15; 4:2
1 Peter 2:2

FAITH WORKS

notes

Chapter Seventeen

Bible Memorization

One of the most thrilling things we can do as Christians is to memorize Scripture. It is easier than you think and will help you to grow as a Christian more quickly and steadily.

Choose verses to memorize based on their personal value to you. One of the first verses I memorized was Ephesians 4:29 because I had a problem with swearing. It was almost an immediate solution!

The easiest way I have found to memorize is to write the verse or verses on one side of a 3x5 card or similar cardstock and the location or "address" on the opposite side. I would try and stick to one verse per card as that will be the verse you will be memorizing. There are times when two verses (or more) may be necessary because one is so short, or it just seems to make more sense.

FAITH WORKS

You have already begun memorizing by writing out the verse. Now read it over carefully and purposefully several times. Next, try to see how much you can remember without looking at the card. You will want to go back and forth between your card and your memory until you can say the verse word perfect without looking at the card. This will probably involve referring back to your card several more times, possibly even for a few days.

It is important to include the address (the location of the verse) when you are memorizing. The best way is probably to recite the address before and after you say the verse. For example: **John 3:16** *For God so loved the world that He gave His only begotten Son, that whoever believes in Him should not perish, but have eternal life.* **John 3:16**

I would begin by memorizing a verse each day following this pattern until you find your comfort level.

CHAPTER SEVENTEEN – BIBLE MEMORIZATION

You need to develop a system for reviewing the verses you memorize as well, or you may forget them or their addresses. You may have to review them daily for a while and then later, when you feel you really know them, you can review them weekly, monthly or whatever works best for you.

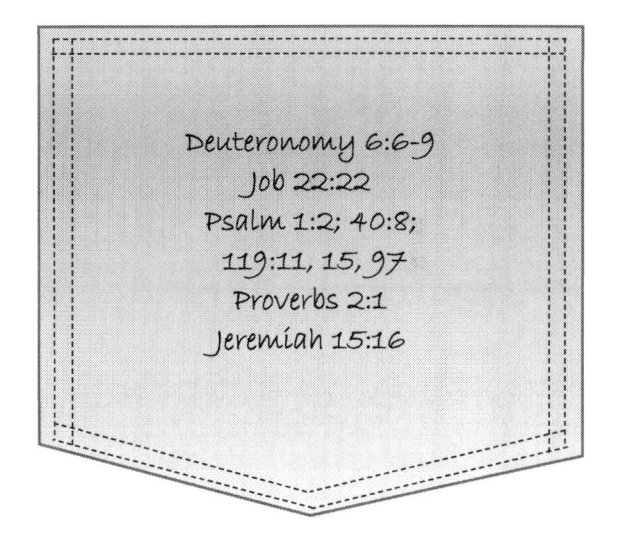

> Deuteronomy 6:6-9
> Job 22:22
> Psalm 1:2; 40:8;
> 119:11, 15, 97
> Proverbs 2:1
> Jeremiah 15:16

FAITH WORKS

notes

Chapter Eighteen

Church

One of the ways we express our love for God and each other is by becoming a part of a local church. When I was a young Christian people told me, "You need to plug into a church." Of course until a person is somewhat settled in a community it will be hard to "plug into" anything.

Selecting a church is going to be one of the most important decisions you ever make. Many people choose to attend a church simply because their family or friends attend there. While this may be a good place to start, you will want to choose a church based on other reasons as well.

First of all you'll need to be sure that the church you attend is a Bible believing church. Does the pastor use his Bible when he preaches? Do the people take their Bibles to church? Do they

FAITH WORKS

honor the Word of God? One word of warning; listen closely to the pastor's teaching. Is he explaining the Bible or simply telling you what to believe. There is a world of difference.

> He has given me a new song to sing, a hymn of praise to our God.
> Psalm 40:3

Another major consideration is music. Does the music honor God? Is it so loud that you cannot hear yourself think? Church is not a rock concert. You are there to worship God. If the music encourages you to truly worship Him that is what is important.

The music should be meaningful to you, but remember the purpose of the music is to please God, not you. Modern music is fine if it allows you to lift your heart and voice to honor God.

Perhaps one of the strongest evidences that we have been born again is that we sing praise to

CHAPTER EIGHTEEN – CHURCH

God. Even people who did not care to sing before they became children of God should now love to sing the praises of God. We sing in order to express love and thanks to God for our salvation. The Bible has many songs interwoven throughout its precious pages. Jesus Himself sang and the angels worship God without ceasing because He is worthy of all praise. It would be hard to imagine a heaven that was not filled with the praise of God in song! We need to get into practice.

Lastly, do the people seem to share a genuine love and concern for each other? You are not there to judge others, but you do have to decide if these are the type of people you want to have for your immediate family. Do they care about the things of God? Do they show an interest in you? Do they encourage

> Your love for one another will prove to the world that you are My disciples.
> John 13:35

FAITH WORKS

you to join in, or do they seem to be comfortable with their own little group? Always try to remember that most people are about as friendly as you are.

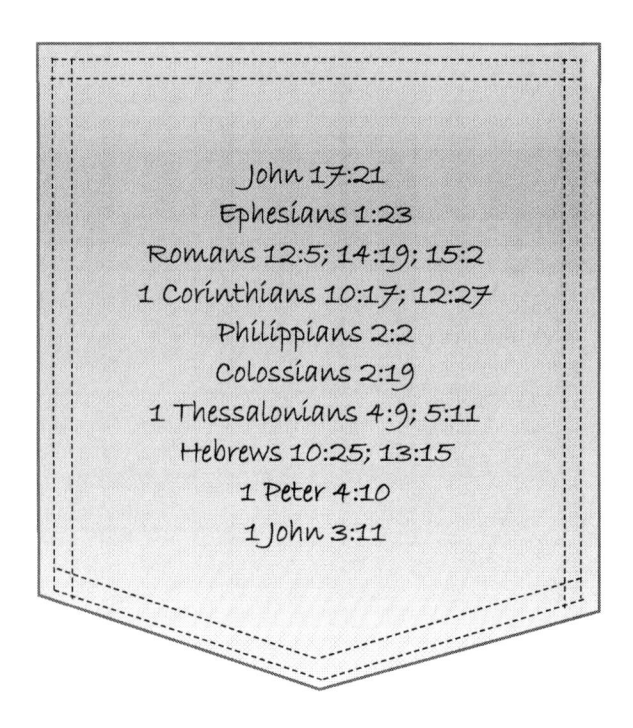

John 17:21
Ephesians 1:23
Romans 12:5; 14:19; 15:2
1 Corinthians 10:17; 12:27
Philippians 2:2
Colossians 2:19
1 Thessalonians 4:9; 5:11
Hebrews 10:25; 13:15
1 Peter 4:10
1 John 3:11

Chapter Nineteen

Work

This is an extremely important matter in our society today. Work is an important part of life. Making an honest living is essential for a Christian.

Laziness is not acceptable for a child of God. It is unsightly in the sight of God. We were created to work, as well as do good works. God did not make us to sit around and watch TV, play games, or drink and smoke ourselves into poor health. Any church that tolerates a person living like this is not living up to Biblical standards. Any Christian who chooses to live this way needs to examine his/herself to see if they truly have been born again. The Holy Spirit does not lead us to live this way.

It is one thing to be unemployed, it is another thing to be lazy. If you do not have a job, your job is to find a job. Once you find a job, do your

FAITH WORKS

best to honor God by working hard for your employer.

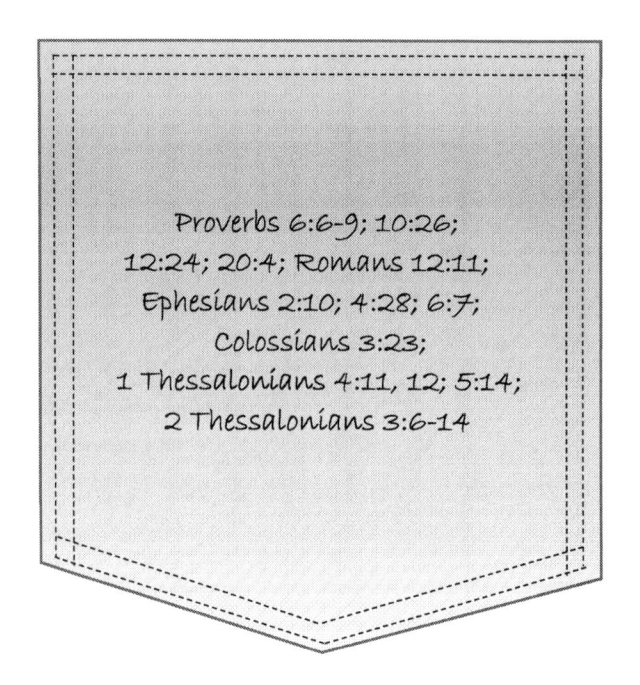

> Proverbs 6:6-9; 10:26;
> 12:24; 20:4; Romans 12:11;
> Ephesians 2:10; 4:28; 6:7;
> Colossians 3:23;
> 1 Thessalonians 4:11, 12; 5:14;
> 2 Thessalonians 3:6-14

Chapter Twenty

Money Matters

What you do with your money matters not only to you but to God as well. He not only knows how many hairs are on your head but how many cents are in your pocket. While we do not think of God as a bookkeeper any more than we think of him as a barber or hairdresser, we must understand that He cares about every detail of our lives. With this in mind, He cares how you spend your money just as much as He cares about how you spend your time. We are to use our money to meet our own needs, the needs of our immediate families, our church family and the work of God throughout the world.

We should never spend more than we earn or we will find ourselves indebted to others. This does not honor God and usually shames us as well. Each person or family should have a budget and stick to that budget. There are a

FAITH WORKS

number of ways to budget, and your pastor should be able to refer you to someone who can help you or guide you to other helpful resources.

Make sure that whatever plan you use, it includes specific plans for giving to the church you attend. Your church will be using those funds to spread the Word of God, the good news about Jesus Christ, the One who has changed your life.

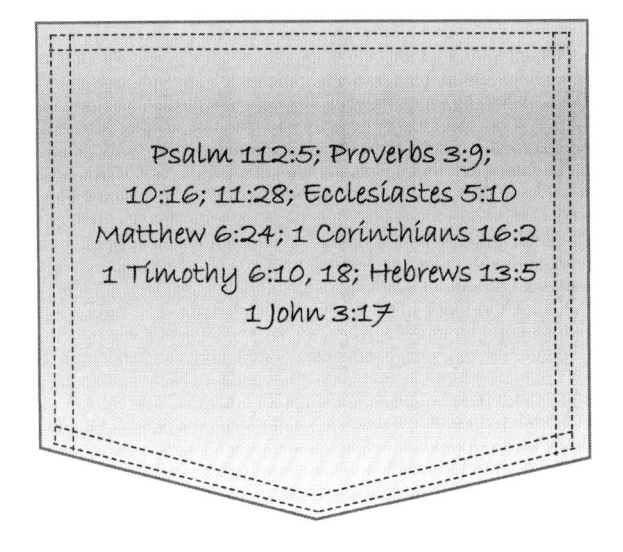

> Psalm 112:5; Proverbs 3:9;
> 10:16; 11:28; Ecclesiastes 5:10
> Matthew 6:24; 1 Corinthians 16:2
> 1 Timothy 6:10, 18; Hebrews 13:5
> 1 John 3:17

Chapter Twenty One

Cults

Be warned, there are false teachers, and there are false churches. They are called cults. When Christians speak of cults they mean groups that are opposed to Christ and Christianity. We mean groups that deny the main teachings of Christianity. There are cults who claim to be Christians, and there are some who clearly deny Christ. The difference is usually what they teach about very basic things like the virgin birth of Christ, His sinless life, His substitutionary death, His resurrection and His future return.

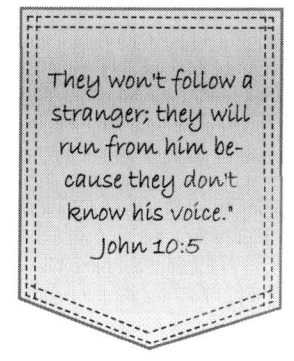

> They won't follow a stranger; they will run from him because they don't know his voice."
> John 10:5

These are not the only ways to identify a cult, but they are a good start. If a group denies that the Bible is the Word of God or requires you to

FAITH WORKS

use a particular Bible (usually with their notes) or requires that you complement your Bible with a special book, they are most probably a cult.

I have been involved in a number of cults myself and thank God that in each case He led me away from them by showing me in the Bible where they were wrong.

I would not advise my path for anyone else. Take the time to learn about any church or group that wants you to join them. If you pray and read the Word of God, He will protect you.

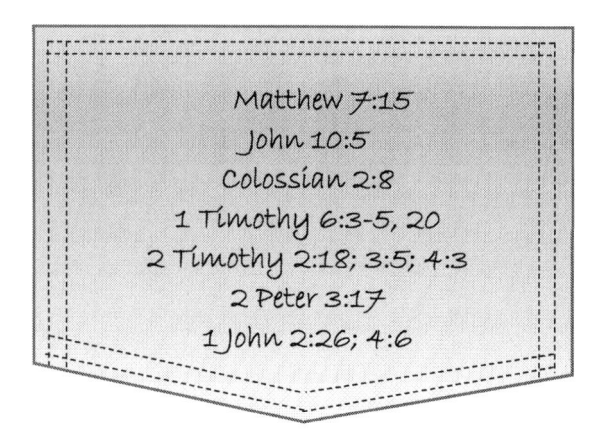

> Matthew 7:15
> John 10:5
> Colossian 2:8
> 1 Timothy 6:3-5, 20
> 2 Timothy 2:18; 3:5; 4:3
> 2 Peter 3:17
> 1 John 2:26; 4:6

Chapter Twenty Two

Spiritual Breathing

One of the first things that we will discover when we walk with God is that we still sin. We have been forgiven but we still have to deal with sin on a daily basis. This requires a constant process of cleansing. The little book of 1 John tells us that, "If we confess our sin He is faithful and just to forgive us and to cleanse us from all unrighteousness." (1 John 1:9) He also reminds us that if we say we have no sin we are only fooling ourselves and refusing to accept the truth. While John probably does not need to tell us that we sin (we all know that we sin), I am glad that He reminds us where our forgiveness comes from.

It would be impractical if not impossible to confess every single sin. But when the Holy Spirit reminds us of our sin, then we need to confess it, agree with God that it is sin and tell Him our desire to be cleansed from all sin.

FAITH WORKS

We call this spiritual breathing; we confess our sins (exhale) and then receive God's forgiveness (inhale). We are not being resaved but we are being renewed. This is often thought of as daily renewal and should be taking place many times each day.

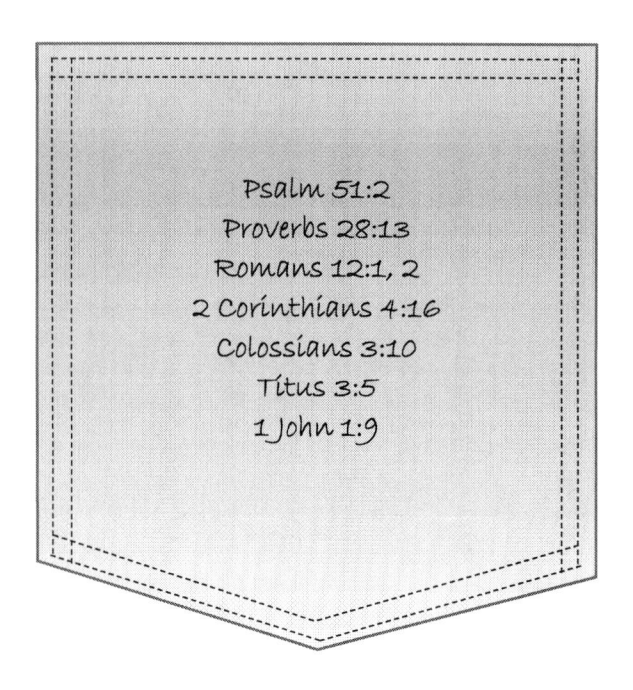

Psalm 51:2
Proverbs 28:13
Romans 12:1, 2
2 Corinthians 4:16
Colossians 3:10
Titus 3:5
1 John 1:9

Chapter Twenty Three

Baptism

One of the first things a new Christian should desire is to be baptized. We are baptized to show others that something of tremendous importance has taken place in our lives. When we go under the water it shows our death and burial (like when Christ died for us), and when we are raised up (as Christ was raised), it reveals that we are new people. It is a symbol of our salvation. We were made clean when our sins were forgiven; when we asked God to forgive us on the basis of the Jesus dying for us. We want others to know that we are new people. It is a testimony to show them that Jesus now lives in us and is at work in the world today.

Baptism is an important step for each Christian and should be desired by every child of God. If you do not want to be baptized, you need to ask yourself why. Jesus Himself was baptized

FAITH WORKS

and left clear instructions that all of His followers were to be taught to be baptized.

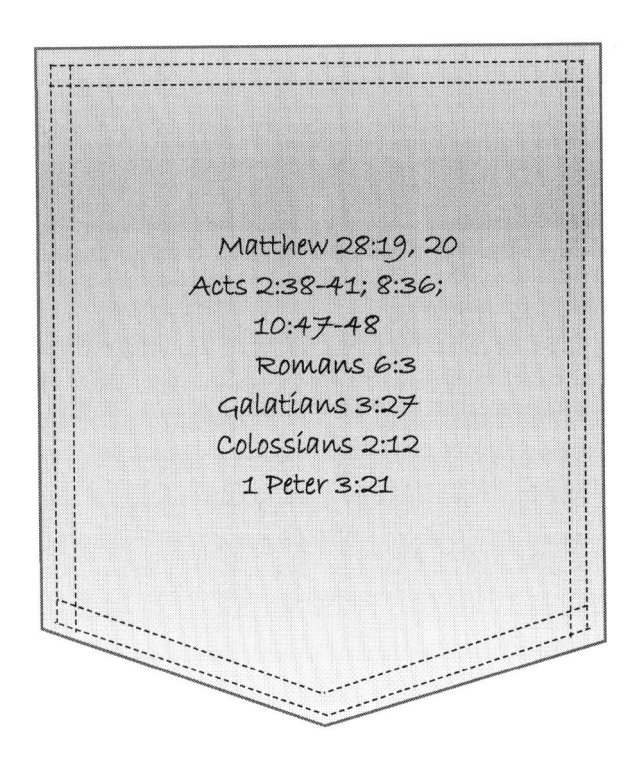

> Matthew 28:19, 20
> Acts 2:38-41; 8:36; 10:47-48
> Romans 6:3
> Galatians 3:27
> Colossians 2:12
> 1 Peter 3:21

Chapter Twenty Four

Backsliding

What does it mean to backslide? It means that you have *purposely* ignored living out the faith that you profess. In your head and your heart you have denied God by your actions. Maybe this is where you are at right now. If so, then this may be your last warning.

If you are God's child, He will not allow you to continue to live in ungodly ways. He loves you so much that He will pluck your life from the earth if you do not return to Him. You must return to Him in repentance and watch Him renew your life day by day. You are not being reborn again. You can only be reborn once. You can, and are supposed to be renewed daily.

Daily renewal calls for daily repentance. If you have been living in sin and calling yourself a Christian, then you need to get alone with God as soon as you possibly can and make sure that

FAITH WORKS

you have confessed your sin and recommitted your life to Him. God does not play games with our spiritual lives. He is more serious than we are, and He knows our hearts.

All sin is serious and has serious consequences. We all sin far more than we are aware of, but to be backslidden means that we are living in sin, not asking for forgiveness and are not trying to please God.

God knows that we are flesh and blood, but He also knows that when we were born again His Holy Spirit came into our lives. The Spirit's presence in our lives enables us to live a life that pleases Him. Even Jesus was tempted. What *is* different about you now is that you have the ability to overcome temptation. You can say "no" because God's Holy Spirit lives in you. You are no different than anyone else in the fact that we are all tempted. We are told in the Bible not to quench the Holy Spirit's desire to work in our lives.

CHAPTER TWENTY FOUR – BACKSLIDING

Luke 21:34
Romans 13:11-14
1 Corinthians 9:24
Galatians 5:7
Ephesians 4:22-24
Philippians 3:13, 14
2 Timothy 2:4
Hebrews 10:37-39; 12:1-4
1 Peter 4:2

FAITH WORKS

notes

Chapter Twenty Five

Two Step Discipleship

Discipleship means following Jesus. When He tells us to act a certain way, we try. When He teaches us what to believe, we believe, whether we fully understand or not. When He reveals how we should be thinking, we try and train ourselves to think this way.

I can think of no clearer explanation of the life of the disciple than to consider two verses in the New Testament.

The first part of step one is found in 2 Corinthians 5:9 which tells us, *we make it our goal to please God*. We need to understand that the goal of discipleship is to bring pleasure to God. Of course we will benefit far more than God will, but God is far more pleased than we are. A prerequisite to being able to please God, however, is that we must search the Scriptures to find out what exactly it is that pleases Him.

FAITH WORKS

This is actually the second part of step one. Ephesians 5:10 says, *find out what pleases the Lord.* These two parts, wanting to please Him and discovering what pleases Him are the first step of discipleship.

The second step is simply to put our feet to the pavement and do those things that we have discovered please Him.

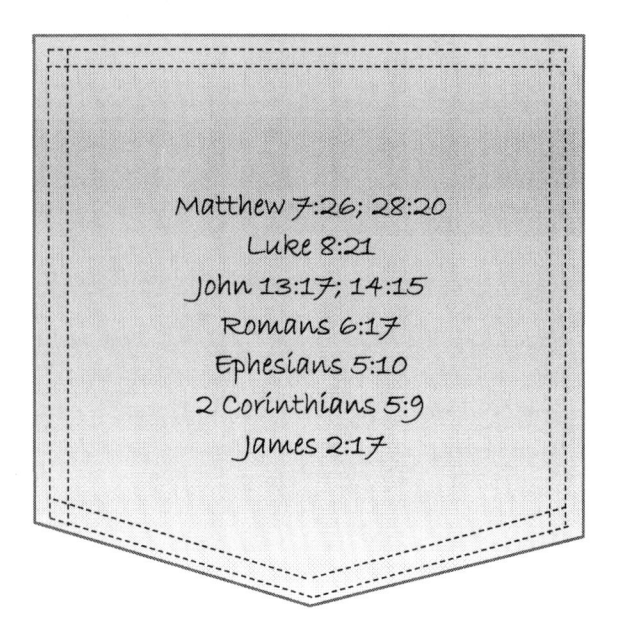

> Matthew 7:26; 28:20
> Luke 8:21
> John 13:17; 14:15
> Romans 6:17
> Ephesians 5:10
> 2 Corinthians 5:9
> James 2:17

Chapter Twenty Six

The Future

Jesus told us not to be overly concerned about the future, either the immediate or the distant. Of course that does not mean that we are never to think about it at all.

There is a wide variety of thinking and preaching when it comes to the future, commonly referred to as the end times. Of one thing we must be sure, Jesus promised to return and to establish His kingdom once and for all.

The church you attend will teach you what they think you need to know about end times. My advice is to be very careful as you try and gain understanding. Many teachers simply tell you what to believe and do not really explain *why* you should believe what they are telling you. Often it is because they do not have a solid understanding themselves. This is not part of the basis of choosing a church, and it is not usually

FAITH WORKS

a very good reason to leave a church. There are exceptions of course.

Every Christian should know that Jesus promised to come again and that when He comes, He will judge the world. To get much beyond this in our understanding will take considerable effort. Your understanding will grow as you grow in the Lord.

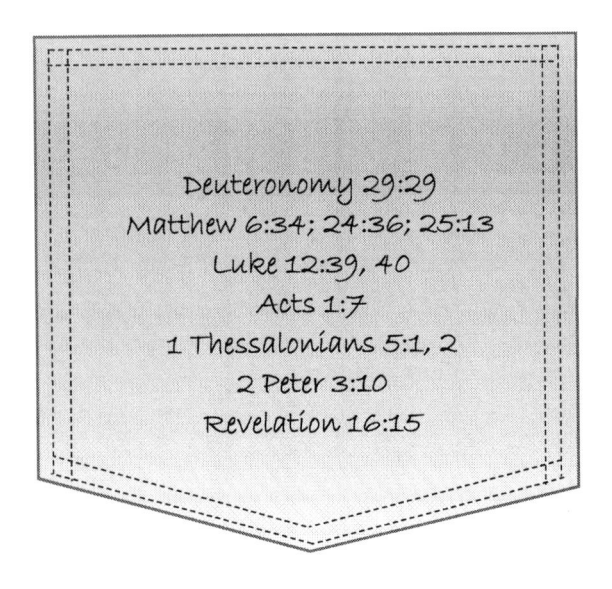

> Deuteronomy 29:29
> Matthew 6:34; 24:36; 25:13
> Luke 12:39, 40
> Acts 1:7
> 1 Thessalonians 5:1, 2
> 2 Peter 3:10
> Revelation 16:15

Meet the Author

Dan Collver has been walking with the Lord Jesus since 1976. He attended Bible college in Portland, Oregon and has an Associate of Arts in Biblical Studies.

In his counterculture experience he stayed at gospel missions from time to time and has a special place in his heart to reach people with the life transforming message of Jesus Christ.

His testimony was aired on Unshackled in 1979 and can be listened to by downloading the QR code on his testimony photo.

"Oh, that we might know the LORD! Let us press on to know Him. He will respond to us as surely as the arrival of dawn or the coming of rains in early spring." Hosea 6:3

notes

"John Doe" is escorted into the Caledonia Court House Wednesday for a bail hearing by Tpr. Dennis Morel (left) and Cpl. Harold Kenney. The defendant was arrested in Norton and has refused to give his name or identification.

ME

A child of rebellion was I, was I,
Looking for answers and questioning why.
I must have the answers, I must understand,
why I was born in this senseless land.

It's a long winding road when you're searching for truth.
I'd heard about Jesus, but I needed more proof.
I'd heard about sin and an eternal hell,
sin sounded like fun, but as for hell, well...

I must taste of sin I thought to myself.
I'll just take a taste of sin off the shelf.
The next thing I knew I was a glutton for sin,
blinded, I feasted, I was taken right in.

I cursed and I laughed and I stole things with glee.
Smoked, drank and made love, I thought I was free.
I lied and I cheated and took LSD
I witnessed for Satan, although ignorantly.

I thought I was God and told others so.
I believed in our God, I just didn't know.
Ever so slowly though God brought me around,
He taught me of Jesus and a new life I've found!

It must have been through the prayers of my mother,
dad, aunts and uncles, my sister and brother.
It must have been through the prayers of my friends,
That Jesus took over and forgave all my sins!

I count them not wasted, those years of my youth,
for now in all honesty I know Jesus as Truth.
Though I wish I'd known sooner our Jesus the Way,
I'm thankful I now know, what more can I say?

Oh, if you're looking for action and are tired of strife,
give my Jesus a try, my Jesus is the Life!

Psalm 19:7   2 Corinthians 5:17